THE
COACH
APPROACH
5 PRINCIPLES TO BUILD
AN E.P.I.C. BUSINESS

THE
COACH
APPROACH

5 PRINCIPLES TO BUILD
AN E.P.I.C. BUSINESS

BILL GILLILAND

FORWARD

Do you have a real business? That's a question I have asked to thousands of business owners just like you in seminars around the world. You see, here at ActionCOACH, my definition of a real business is a "Commercial, Profitable Enterprise that Works, Without You." The "without you" part is the bit that challenges most people in business.

In my book, *The Business Coach,* I outline the 6 steps to build a business. What we've found from coaching business owners to greater success is that when business people (with the assistance of their ActionCOACH) follow the six steps, they make the transition from operator to "coach" of their own businesses. This final step frees them to live the life they always dreamed about, to own multiple businesses, to "cash out", or just do the fun things in their businesses.

Bill Gilliland, the author of this book has made a career (he calls it a calling) of working with people in business - coaching them up the ladder to business success. His clients regularly make this transition to become "coaches" of their own businesses.

Furthermore, Bill is not just another coach who has never owned a business. In addition to his coaching business, Bill has owned several businesses in industries ranging from automotive to automation, and from retail to transportation.

Drawing on years of actual coaching experience, owning multiple businesses, learning from other ActionCOACHes, and by studying athletic coaches such as the great John Wooden, Bill noticed certain commonalities that applied to all coaching and success. Out of this came the 4 EPIC building blocks of a coaching program and 5 overriding coaching principles to be applied in your business.

This book and the accompanying workbook will give you both the theoretical and practical steps you need to move you and your business to the next level. If you'll do the work, this book will give you the keys to unlock the business of your dreams.

All the Best!

Brad Sugars
Chairman and CEO
ActionCOACH

DEDICATION

To my Parents

This book is dedicated to my parents, Jack and Marian Gilliland who were and are the ultimate "coaches" in my life. They showed me that only leadership by example is real leadership.

TABLE OF CONTENTS

Forward 5

Acknowledgments 11

Introduction 13

Chapter 1 The People Development Business 15

Chapter 2 The Coach Confidence Cycle 17

Chapter 3 The Four EPIC Building Blocks 23

Chapter 4 EPIC Principle #1: You're So Fine... 29

Chapter 5 EPIC Principle #2: To Have EPIC Wins, You
Must Have EPIC Fails 33

Chapter 6 EPIC Principle #3: The Numbers Don't Lie. 39

Chapter 7 EPIC Principle #4: It's About Them 47

Chapter 8 Epic Principle #5 - Relationships Matter 59

Chapter 9 Conclusion 63

About the Author 67

ACKNOWLEDGMENTS

First of all, thank you to my wife, Lynn, who has supported and put up with my entrepreneurial endeavors for over 30 years. Thanks to my sons, Mac and Matthew, who have learned to follow Rule #1 and the rest of the rules.

Writing and publishing a book doesn't just happen. It takes a team. Thanks to:

All of my clients. You know who you are, and you know what you mean to me. You have my eternal gratitude. I've learned more from you than I'll ever be able to teach you.

Brad Sugars, the founder and CEO of ActionCOACH . Thank you for creating a company and a platform that makes it possible for me to be in the coaching business. You are one of my greatest mentors and have truly taught me what it means to be a coach.

Steve Leach. You have forgotten more than most of us know. I appreciate your leadership, guidance, and friendship.

All of the ActionCOACHes and the entire ActionCOACH community who have inspired and helped me along my journey. Specifically I'd like to thank Monte Wyatt who taught me about KPIs, Iain Mcfarlane who taught me what it means to be congruent, Jody Johnson, who makes me laugh, and my late business partner, Johnny Barr, who put up with a lot as we learned the coaching business. Johnny taught me a lot about trust, the numbers, and recognizing greatness. Additionally, I'd like to thank the North

Carolina team; specifically Reggie Shropshire, Ross Cox, and Steve Brock who have helped me with "market research."

Beverly Buckner and Katie Locke. You've both contributed in ways you can never imagine.

My editor, Katie Chambers of Beacon Publishing. She's a rock star and did an amazing job. http://beaconpointservices.org

My sister, Jean Levett, who proofed the manuscript. She's also a rock star in the world of details.

My brother John, for being my brother.

Happy Self Publishing for the amazing cover and the formatting. http://www.happyselfpublishing.com.

Mr. Tim Templeton for developing the business-relational matrix and writing the book *The Referral of a Lifetime.*

And my last acknowledgment goes to Coach John Wooden. I never had the opportunity to meet Coach Wooden, but a great coach leaves a legacy of players and coaches. He is still impacting me and millions of people around the world. Thanks, Coach!

INTRODUCTION

Most entrepreneurs and business owners I meet have at least some element of "control freak" as part of their makeup. Some of us even fall into the "certified control freak" category. That means we know we are control freaks but don't know how to change by ourselves.

It makes sense really. After all, as entrepreneurs and business owners, we put in long hours to make our businesses successful.

We master the basics, find our niche, build out systems, and find and develop great team members. Just when we are hitting our strides, we realize that in order to keep growing, we have to let go of the reins and watch someone else run "our baby."[1] This reluctance to let go is silly, given that when we do our jobs right, we have employed great people who are actually better than we are at running the day-to-day operations of our businesses.

In this book, you'll learn the principles that will allow you to remain in charge, but not in control. At least not in control of the day-to-day running of your business. And you'll learn how to run your business in less than half a day per week. As Sir Richard Branson says, "If you can learn how to run one business successfully, then there is no reason you can't run any number of businesses at the same time . . . . The principles are still the same."

---

[1] In order to reach a point where you can consider taking a "coach approach" with your business, I recommend that you read and apply The 6 Steps to Grow a Business as outlined in *The Business Coach* by Brad Sugars. Or better yet, read the book and work with an ActionCOACH to get you there.

If you are a business owner having a hard time letting go, a manager interested in coaching rather than bossing your team, or someone just interested in knowing how to implement a coaching program inside your business, then you are in the right place. Keep reading.

While working with business owners for over a decade, I discovered our best clients worked their way out of their businesses and essentially became "coaches" for their businesses. Coaching, instead of managing, allowed them to run multiple businesses, devote more time to their families, and have energy to give back to their communities.

In analyzing how they made this last jump from general manager to "coach," I began to notice a set of common principles and a framework that could be replicated. This set of generalized principles is "The Coach Approach," which allows you to create an **EPIC** business.

When you use the four EPIC building blocks and the five EPIC principles outlined in this book, and the framework in its companion workbook, you will learn how to stay in charge, but not in control; build your business or multiple businesses; and finally find the freedom that attracted or drove you into running a business in the first place. You'll learn how to coach your people to run your business for you, and in turn, they'll help you build the life you said you'd live. The "Coach Approach" will get you there. You can "Be EPIC".

So go ahead and get started. Read through the book quickly the first time. Then read it again to lock in the principles—so you can begin coaching, give up some control, stay in charge, and build the business and life of your dreams.

Please download the workbook that accompanies this book at https://billgilliland.biz/epicworkbook

CHAPTER 1

THE PEOPLE DEVELOPMENT BUSINESS

A few months ago, one of my clients said he believed he wasn't in the excavation business; he was actually in the people development business. He's right. All of us are in the people development business. In order to grow your business, your people will need to develop and grow first.

In his book, *The 21 Irrefutable Laws of Leadership*, John Maxwell describes the "Law of the Lid." The Law of the Lid states that the business can only grow to the level of the leader's capabilities. So by taking a coach approach, we give our teams more freedom, responsibility, and room for growth. This increases your capacity for leadership: your lid. When you raise your lid, you raise your company's lid.[2]

Business owners must have patience and invest time in developing their people. It seems that business owners and managers have short-term amnesia. They forget the mistakes they made in the early

---

[2] Maxwell, John C. *The 21 Irrefutable Laws of Leadership: Follow Them and People Will Follow You*. Nashville, TN: Thomas Nelson, 1-10.

days of their careers. Maybe they are in a hurry, lack patience, or fear the surprise of hearing how someone on their team messed up something. I've heard every worry.

As we give our employees more responsibility and more freedom, they will make mistakes and they will do things differently than the way we would have done them. Just like a child learning to walk, they will fall down. You wouldn't say to that child, "Stay down; you must be one of the non-walkers." You instead say, "Get up and try again and again until you get it right."

With freedom comes responsibility and the opportunity to succeed or fail. Remember in business, failure is not necessarily a bad thing. In fact, it's a good thing. Failure is not the opposite of success—it is a part of success. In most cases, it's the rate at which we learn from our failures that determines our success. The faster we fail (work out what doesn't work), the faster we find success.

Investing time and money developing your people is worth it, because as you invest in them, your team becomes more engaged in your vision and your enterprise. An engaged team becomes easier to manage, gets better results, earns mores profits, and creates more time for you to contribute back to your team and to your community.

Later in the book, I will go into the various coaching styles in great detail. Suffice it to say your coaching style should be based on who you are and not someone you are trying to emulate. You may be tempted to copy someone else's coaching style, but you can't be someone else. Find your coaching style and make it work for you.

I have a friend whom I admire very much and who is a very charismatic coach. In my early days, I copied his language and his style. Because it wasn't my style, what worked for him sounded disingenuous to my clients. I learned to understand the context (his intent) of his style and develop my own content (words, language, and style) to make it work for me.

CHAPTER 2

THE COACH CONFIDENCE CYCLE

Relationships build results, results raise retention. Better retention makes recruitment easier, which in turn starts the cycle over by building even better relationships. So let's look at each one of these individually.

The Coach Confidence Cycle

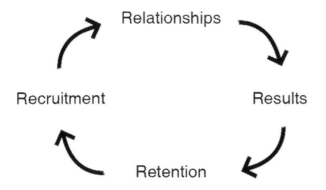

Relationships: A Few Notes on a Healthy Coaching Relationship

When you hire an athletic or personal trainer, their number one goal is to push you to get the results you said you wanted. The trainer is not necessarily your friend, your buddy, or Mr. or Ms. Nice Guy. Their job is to get you to wherever you said you wanted to go by whatever means it takes to get you there.

If you want to train for a 5K race, you'll get a very different training experience than a world-class athlete looking to make the Olympic team. Each person is different, has different aims and skills, and each needs an individual approach.

Great coaches take this individual approach while maintaining an eye on the overall team goals. A great football coach might have to be very upbeat and inspirational with one member of the team, and then walk over and scream and yell at another member to get that person fired up.

Each person responds to different stimuli and different styles. How well one can relate to and interact with each team member's individual preferences and styles indicates how successful they will be. My basketball coach in high school was a genius at knowing which buttons to push. He generally went "old school" with me and got in my face, letting me know exactly how it felt because he knew that approach worked well with me. With another teammate, who would have crumpled in the face of criticism, he took a more inspirational approach. At all times, he worked to make us better individually. Only as better individuals could we contribute to making the team better.

To build an **EPIC** business, you will need to take this individual/team approach. A healthy coaching relationship is built on respect for each other, on having clear goals that you've both agreed upon, and on doing whatever it takes to push the person to reach those goals. You may or may not become friends. In this case, friendship is not the key metric to achieve—getting results is what matters most.

I find it useful to use the metaphor of differing "hats." In your life, you wear multiple hats. When you are coaching, you will have your "coach hat" on. If you go into friend mode, you will put your "friend hat" on. As a manager, you'll put your "manager hat" on. And so on. The challenge and the trick is to be very clear with other people which hat you have on at all times. If you switch from coach to friend, before moving on, you must stop and say to the person, "I'm putting my friend hat on now."

The coaching relationship will likely become intimate—even with employees. You will know things about the person you're coaching that you will learn in confidence. In order to create trusting relationships, be prepared to hear some things or stories you aren't expecting.

For example, I had a client who said to me, "Bill, I've just got to tell someone. I'm pregnant again."

I said, "Who knows other than your husband and doctor?"

"That would be you. It's too early to tell the world and I knew you would keep a secret." I was honored and proud. When you keep their trust, your people will want to grow, and your team will get better.

Results

As you build better business relationships, you'll find that your teams will get better results. As you achieve those better results, you'll have more profit and you'll have more time. Studies in large companies have borne this out. In an article for Forbes.com, Joseph Folkman cites a study his company did in a large energy company.

"One important attribute we find in employees who have great leaders is 'their willingness to go the extra mile.'" In the same study they also "found that employees were not only more productive, but good coaching also improved their engagement."[3] Relationships go hand in hand with results.

Retention

Back in the 1960s, my grandfather said that the younger generation was "going to hell," and later my Dad wondered what was going to happen with my generation,[4] and now all the talk is about "millennials."

In my opinion, this generational stereotyping is mostly bunk. Every generation has hard working, successful people; and every generation has deadbeats.

You've probably heard or read millennials are addicted to electronics, they jump from job to job, and businesspeople must learn how to deal with them.

In reality, the job-hopping trend is nothing new. It's not a millennial thing; it's a people thing. It's a rarity to meet anyone who has stayed in one job for their entire career. So let's acknowledge that employee retention is hard and getting more difficult. Creating stronger relationships can slow down or potentially reverse this trend. And better results will increase retention. Most of the studies I have seen correlate poor retention with poor results.

My contention is that it works both ways. If an employee gets great results, they are most likely happier and earning more. And people who are happier and earning more are more likely to stick around. It

---

[3] Folkman, Joseph. "5 Business Payoffs for Being an Effective Coach." *Forbes*, February 19, 2015.
[4] I'm in the tail end of "The Baby Boomers."

becomes a nice self-fulfilling prophesy that continues as the Coach Approach helps teams get better results and retention improves.

Recruitment

The top athletic teams in the country don't really have to recruit since recruits want to play for those coaches and teams (such as Duke or North Carolina in basketball, and Alabama or Clemson in football). They want to become part of that tradition. The recruits just show up. As you build a great team and a great culture, employees or potential employees will begin showing up.

Southwest Airlines gets an employment application about every two seconds because it's a cool place to work since they build great relationships, get great results, and have fun. In an environment like that, employees tend to stick around.

And with all those applications, what does Southwest Airlines get to do? They get to choose the best people! It's like fishing with a net versus fishing with a single hook. When I fly fish, I generally use one fly with one hook. Most of the time I "catch and release" the fish I catch. If I were fishing for food, I'd have to decide whether or not each fish is big enough to keep. A commercial fisherman catches a net full of fish, making it easier to decide which fish are too small and need to go back into the water. Southwest Airlines can keep the best fish.

Is your business to a point where it gets to keep only the best fish? Are people knocking your doors down to come to work with you, or do you still have to invest tons of money and time looking for employees?

Build relationships, get results, improve retention, and get ready to have your pick of the best applicants.

CHAPTER 3

THE FOUR EPIC BUILDING BLOCKS

When I saw my best clients make the transition from manager to coach in their businesses, I wondered if there was a set path or methodology that other owners and managers could follow. EPIC is that framework. What I found was that to be successful in making that transition to "coach," people needed to work within four EPIC building blocks.

"Formal education will make you a living. Self-education will make you a fortune."
Jim Rohn

E is for Education

Question: How many books are in the libraries? Answer: All of them.

"Education" is derived from the same word as "educe," which means to draw out and implies bringing out of someone something greater, generally a potential or something latent. Coaching at its finest brings out potential and something latent in people. Any coaching program has to have education as a key component.

Education includes the personal improvement plan (PIP), which is designed to give the person a life path; and a professional development plan (PDP), which is designed to assist in furthering a person's career. See more about these in the workbook.

Elements of both of these plans may include any or all of the following: books, videos, audios, seminars, classes, etc. It will depend on the individual's personal learning preferences and budget to determine which elements will go into their plans.

"The value of planning is not necessarily in the plan; it's in the planning."
Bill Gilliland

P is for Planning.

In hundreds of seminars, I've asked participants "Why don't people plan?" I've heard all kinds of answers: fear of failure, fear of success, lazy, not enough time, scared, don't know how, it might not work. They're all excuses. I don't accept excuses. Because when I ask the same people "Do you believe that planning is important?" they all say "yes." So planning is the second key component of any successful coaching program.

I advocate a 5/3/1/90 goal setting and planning approach. What that means is you build a five-year comprehensive plan; and to help you get there, you build a three-year set of milestones, a one-year plan, and a quarterly or ninety-day plan.

People ask me all the time "why ninety days?" Ninety days is long enough to get something done and short enough to keep your eye on the ball. One year or five years is just too long for most people to stay focused. Have you ever done a one-year plan, set it on the shelf, and then in about November you come back and look at it and say, "Yeah, okay, how am I doing?"

Ninety-day plans eliminate that. A quarterly plan is divided into thirteen weekly plans. This simple action of "chunking down" your plan into manageable steps guarantees movement towards your long term goals.

In the last week of every quarter, you will review your progress and complete another ninety-day plan. Once a quarterly plan is in place, it becomes easier to hold the people you coach accountable to the plan. The accompanying workbook has an entire module on planning.

"Success is peace of mind which is a direct result of self-satisfaction in knowing you made the effort to become the best of which you are capable."
Coach John Wooden

I is for Inspiration

Have you ever heard of a good coach, a good symphony conductor, or a theater director who wasn't able to inspire their teams, their musicians, or their casts? Of course not. They were able to stir emotions and get them to perform at a higher level. Coaching business people is the same.

Inspiration starts with *why* and ends with *vision*. As a leader, you must enthusiastically and clearly articulate your vision, your team's mission, and why they are important. Simon Sinek, in his famous TED Talk titled "How Great Leaders Inspire Action," says that "People don't buy what you do. They buy why you do it." If you have not already seen it, please stop reading and go watch the TED Talk now.

Once you are clear on your *why* and your *vision*, invest some of your time with your team finding out which parts of your why and your vision resonate with them. When you understand what makes them come to work every day, you'll be on the road to keeping them engaged. It'll be a lot easier to inspire already engaged people. It doesn't mean that they will be positive all the time. From time to time, you'll still have to push, pull, poke, prod, demand, and do whatever it takes to keep them going.

Have you ever had anyone say to you, "you'll figure it out"? And you think or say, "Thanks for nothing!" Well, this is one of those times that you must learn from doing. You'll figure it out. Get started working on your why and your vision. The workbook has exercises to get you started.

It is important to maintain congruence in a coaching relationship. I have found that the coaching relationship provides a direct and clear communication feedback loop between two people. In contrast, the feedback that I get from a prospective client in a sales situation may be filtered, because my prospect will not likely share all of the relevant information with me. I have to guess and deduce. A coaching feedback loop is like a mirror, giving me instant and accurate feedback.

You will get crystal clear feedback from the people you coach. The moment you spot you are having trouble coaching your coachee; you can figure out why and apply that feedback. For example, if you're having trouble inspiring the people you coach to write a plan, it's probably because you don't have a written plan. You don't have to be miles ahead of your reports, but you do have to be a step or two ahead.

To fully take *The Coach Approach*, to be inspirational, you have to "drink your own Kool-Aid" and do what you teach. You must be congruent.

"The only failure is the failure to participate."
Brad Sugars

C is for Commitment.

For *The Coach Approach* to work, you must make your coaching program one of your top three priorities. Otherwise, it's just another initiative that'll end up in the waste bin.

People who don't want or resist coaching will eventually get their wish, and they'll either be out of the coaching program or they'll actually be out of a job because they don't want to grow. Both parties in a coaching relationship must commit.

A large part of commitment is consistency. You will want to establish rules to ensure consistency:

- Coach on a weekly or bi-weekly schedule.
- Schedule coaching sessions on a regular day at a regular time.
- Have the same format and script at each session.
- Take great notes.
- Measure everything.

Come ready to play at 100% because you already know that whatever you put into something, you get back out. The workbook covers this in more detail.

Action Step: On a scale of 1 to 10 what's your commitment level?

The four EPIC building blocks are needed to apply the five EPIC principles that will guide your transition to *The Coach Approach*.

"The most beautiful thing you can wear is confidence."
- Blake Lively

CHAPTER 4

EPIC PRINCIPLE #1: YOU'RE SO FINE...

I grew up and still live in the southern part of the United States—
"The South." So, I like big breakfasts: Eggs, grits, bacon,
biscuits . . . you get the picture. These days that kind of food is more
of a treat. We, as a society, know too much. We worry about how
food affects us, so I'm more health conscious (most of the time).
Now, I'm more of a yogurt, cereal, and fruit kind of guy.

Once I was in San Francisco wandering along the bay shopping in
an open-air market looking for some breakfast things to have in my
room so I wouldn't have to pay big bucks for a breakfast. Breakfast
items I would love, but wouldn't make me feel fat.

I found an eight-foot high display of every variety of trail mix you
could imagine. I was just trying to get the regular kind of trail mix,
the peanut, raisin, chocolate candies variety. Because the grocers
were good retailers and had the exotic, high end, more expensive
trail mixes at eye level, the regular trail mix was near the bottom of
the rack.

A lady had her back to me kneeling down also searching for something near the bottom of the rack. In order to get the regular variety of trail mix, I had to reach over and around her. It was a little awkward, but I was on a mission to get my breakfast supplies.

As I reached over and around her to grab the bag of trail mix, she said, "Excuse me." I said, "You're fine," which is Southern for "you don't need to move. You are okay staying right where you are."

It might not have translated well into Californian. But she looked up at me and said, "Yes, I **am**." It wasn't arrogant or vain. It was confident and attractive. I thought and maybe said out loud, "Wow." Looking back, I wished I had asked her a few more questions so I could find out where she got (and how she kept) that high level of confidence.

I haven't been able to get that incident out of my head because, that's the level of confidence that EPIC coaches need. You have to believe—no, you must know—you are making a difference in your clients' or team members' lives. You are helping them see what they can't see, change what they need to change, and become the person they are capable of becoming.

Life changed for me when in a coaching session one of my coaches said, "Bill, you are one of the best coaches on the planet." After thinking about it for a few minutes, you know what I said? "Yes, I am."

You should say it right now out loud, too: "I am one of the greatest coaches on the planet. I am one of the greatest coaches on the planet."

Action Step:

Add "I am . . . " statements around points of confidence to your routine every day. Say them out loud with emotion twice daily.

Examples: "I am one of the greatest coaches on the planet." "I am confident and strong and getting better every day."

Make a list of 10 "I am . . . " statements and say them aloud with emotion twice daily: once in the morning and once right before bed.

"Most people have attained their greatest success just one step beyond their greatest failure."
- Napoleon Hill.

CHAPTER 5

EPIC PRINCIPLE #2: TO HAVE EPIC WINS, YOU MUST HAVE EPIC FAILS

When I was in college, some of us got the bright idea to earn extra money for the fraternity. I don't remember our exact motivation, but we probably wanted to throw another party.

We saw some other guys selling painter's hats before a basketball game for a couple of dollars each. They sold out. We did some quick math, and Holy Cow! By our calculations, these guys made a few thousand dollars—in about two hours.

We thought, *we can do that*. At the time, The Pittsburgh Steelers of the National Football League had just come out with The Terrible Towel. Pittsburgh is football crazy, and the fans couldn't buy them fast enough. We went to Duke, a great basketball school with crazy fans, and we thought, *they'll buy anything*.

So we decided to sell a small version of the towel. I was in charge of the project. Although we got permission from the school to use the design, I think we had to pay a percentage to them. No worries; we were all going to be rich! I contracted with a company to make the towels. We put all of our money into the project. After all, we were going to get rich!

However, we ran into a few problems: First, the product actually manufactured looked more like a handkerchief than a towel. Second, the color was all wrong—the color turned out to be pretty close to Carolina's blue, and not Duke's blue. Duke is dark blue; Carolina is sky blue. If you know anything about basketball or rivalries, Duke and Carolina (UNC-Chapel Hill) are located only eleven miles apart and have the most famous rivalry in college basketball, and in some opinions, the best rivalry in all of sport.

We tried everything to sell those "handkerchiefs." We had the cheerleaders wear and wave them. We sold them two for one. But we couldn't give them away. Yes, we learned the hard way. Yes, we got a great education. Yes, I still have one of those handkerchiefs. And I still can't give it away. Nor would I. It's a great reminder of how far and how fast I have grown.

We failed because we didn't plan and because we didn't know what we were doing. Or at least I didn't know what I was doing. If we had taken time to plan, we would have learned what we needed to do to find success.

At the time, I was book smart, but not business smart. You are not going to be great at anything the first time you try it. You didn't ride a bike the first time you tried without training wheels. I'm sure you missed the basket on your first basketball shot. You couldn't play the violin or the piano the first time you tried. I remember clearly that I completely missed the ball on my first golf swing. And I certainly didn't know anything about making money the first time I tried a business deal.

While the experience may have seemed like a failure, it ended up being a great investment in learning. I learned to do market research before a product launch and to test and measure everything.

If I had proactively found mentors and coaches earlier, I would have achieved more earlier on. But I learned through my experiences, and now I feel honored that I get to teach others what I did to find success and what to avoid so they don't make the same mistakes I made.

The best in the world, the smartest people in the world, agree that in order for you to move forward, you must fail. In fact, they agree you have to fail regularly, and you have to fail faster than anyone else.

The world works in a continuum, but for practical purposes, it appears to be two-sided. You can't have up without down, you can't have left without right, and you can't have success without failure. In other words, the faster you can fail forward, the more successes you are likely to find.

Let's say you are in sales. In order to succeed, you have to get "yesses," right? But since you can't possibly sell everyone, you will get some "noes" and "yesses," and because sales is a numbers game, the key to getting more "yesses" is getting more "noes."

So go out and get more "noes." See how many you can get. Make a game of it. Fail miserably. Along the way, you'll find some "yesses" and you'll find success. Enjoy the ride!

Coaching is the same. You don't have to be perfect—not everything will work out. Remember, you are not a genius, a guru, or a robot. You are a person. You are a human. You will make mistakes. Make sure your coachee knows that they too will make mistakes. Not everything your coachee will try will work for them.

I once coached a man who wanted to hire a general manager for his team. He did everything right. He was clear on the type of person he wanted and what he expected the person to do. He marketed well and found a number of qualified candidates. Through a series of interviews and demonstrations, he picked the best candidate. The candidate was great, and he did a great job for three months.

In the end, although he'd been living locally for some time, he was homesick for his hometown, and he went home. Even when you do everything right, not everything works out. Learn and move on.

Failure is inevitable, but not **permanent**. Plan, measure, test, and improve.

One of the greatest lessons I have learned while being a coach came from one of my mentors, Brad Sugars, the founder of ActionCOACH. In business, like baseball, measure everything. Then make small changes, re-measure, adjust, re-test, and keep improving.

It looks something like a reverse G. See the diagram below.

Reverse "G" Test and Measure

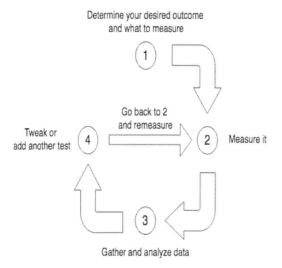

At the top of the *G*, at point one, find something you want to measure and determine the outcome you'd like to have. At number two on the downward part of the *G*, measure that item. At number three, the bottom of the *G*, gather and analyze the data, and then at number four, tweak it. From there, shoot across to the measurement stage and see whether, once you measure it again, the outcome got better or worse.

If it was better, then maybe you test another assumption. If it was worse, then go back to the original condition, and try something else. Continuously go around in this circle, in this reverse *G*, making improvements until you reach a point where you like the outcomes you are getting.

"You can't play the game without keeping score."

CHAPTER 6

EPIC PRINCIPLE #3:
THE NUMBERS DON'T LIE.[5]

Building Your Scorecard

Baseball loves statistics. They have on base percentage, slugging percentage, earned run average (ERA), pitch counts, how many times a certain batter gets a hit with two strikes when he is thrown a curve ball, how often a player gets on base with his mother in the stands, etc. Baseball tracks everything, and baseball can teach those of us in business a lot about using tracking and statistics.

The movie *Moneyball*,[6] based on the book by Michael Lewis, chronicles the unlikely trip of the Oakland Athletics to The American League Championship Series in 2002. With the third lowest payroll in baseball, the Oakland A's are forced to look at

[5] This chapter is largely based on a talk that my friend and colleague, Monte Wyatt, gave at the Business Excellence Forum in Orlando, Florida, on February 24, 2016. Used with Permission.
[6] *Moneyball* is a 2011 American film based on Michael Lewis's 2003 nonfiction book of the same name. It's an account of the Oakland Athletics' 2002 season and their general manager Billy Beane's attempts to assemble a competitive team.

baseball through a different lens than other teams in the league. Some, like the New York Yankees, had as much as three times the money to invest in players' payroll. They needed to determine what to focus on that would make the difference between a winning and a losing season.

The A's in 2002 had a problem. After a successful 2001 season, the team lost three of their key players through free agency to other teams in the league. Conventional wisdom said go out and buy other players, but the team could not afford similar players.

Peter Grant, a young recent graduate of Yale, goes against all conventional baseball wisdom and teaches Billy Beane, the manager of the Oakland Athletics, a different way to look at the statistics. Beane, who is smart— having given up a scholarship to Stanford to pursue a career in professional baseball — buys into Grant's premise.

Grant believed in order to get more runs, and ultimately more wins, the team needed players with a high "on base percentage." Conventional scouts looked at batting averages, stolen bases, runs batted in, etc. Among all the myriad of other offensive statistics that the baseball gurus love to track, Peter believed the only one that mattered was did the player get on base. And furthermore, it didn't matter how they got on base.

In business, we call a statistic like this a Key Performance Indicator—or KPI. It is a number that when tracked and improved will improve an outcome. If a player gets on base more times, he's more likely to score more runs. More runs equals more wins. The concept is simple. And Billy Beane bought into the simplicity, even though his coaches and scouts did not. He really had no choice because he just didn't have the payroll of the "richer" teams like The NY Yankees.

Billy Beane looked for and signed players with high on base percentages, but who were undervalued by other teams because the other teams looked at other statistics. In doing so, Billy Beane and The Oakland Athletics changed baseball forever.

Get Creative

Have you ever noticed when you find yourself with a problem, or in a "jam" or a "tight spot," you become creative and often find a different path or solution to your issue?

I once worked with an attorney who just couldn't quite get his billings to where he needed or wanted them to be. In the legal world, the normal measure of productivity is billable hours. Attorneys track the hours they work on their clients' cases and then bill them at their hourly rate.

Some attorneys also take certain kinds of work based on a fixed fee. We tried converting the fixed fee jobs into billable hours and also tracked the hourly jobs. The tracking process was confusing, and it simply didn't work for him. We tried several productivity strategies and nothing improved.

Then, we took another approach. Since his end goal was earning more money, we worked out how much money he wanted to make in a year, figured out how much he actually needed to bill in dollars per day each day he worked, and tracked that. Voila, he easily surpassed his dollar billing goals.

For him "billable hours" was a nebulous number. It meant nothing. "Dollars billed" was very clear to him. Now, he had the one KPI to track—dollars billed per day.

So how do we find the numbers we most need to track? There's usually one specific thing. Find that answer. What is the one KPI that's most important to track? In most businesses, it's a productivity number. It's something like gross profit per hour or like my attorney, dollars billed per day. Each position will have a different KPI. For a salesperson, it might be appointments booked per week. For a production manager, it might be number of widgets safely produced per day.

Use this process to find your number(s):

1. Identify a problem to solve, an opportunity that you can leverage, or something you want to improve.
2. Set the outcome to be achieved and the action to take.
3. Track it. Chart the progress and execution.
4. Select the leading and lagging KPI's (leading and lagging are explained below) that you want to look at, preferably daily.
5. Set the accountability and a method to report.

To find your numbers, you need to know the types of indicators.

Leading indicators. Leading Indicators are numbers or activities that when improved will lead to an improved outcome. For example, if a salesperson is looking to get more leads, then she should track the number of hours per day spent prospecting or the number of networking events she attended. Of course, number of leads obtained might be a leading indicator for sales dollars earned. Other examples of leading indicators are number of appointments booked, number of conversations with prospects, and actual time spent with prospects.

Lagging indicators. Lagging Indicators are what we want to track but they are outcomes of other activities or numbers. For example the number of new customers our salesperson gains is a lagging indicator because it is the product of other inputs—the number of leads she gets multiplied by the rate at which she converts those leads into customers. Other examples of lagging indicators are revenues and net profits.

People indicators. People indicators measure how a person, team, or company is performing. These numbers can be subjective and are obtained through surveys or observations. For example, a number measuring how much our salesperson's clients enjoy buying from her. Examples of people indicators are measures of customer satisfaction, client retention, and employee engagement.

Productivity indicators. Productivity Indicators are an outcome divided by an input. For our salesperson, a productivity indicator would be the number of sales made per sales meeting. The number of sales would be the output and the number of sales meetings would be the input. Examples of other productivity indicators are sales per hour, gross profit per labor hour, and return on investment.

The Process

All people want to know how they are doing. They need a scoreboard. A Key Performance Indicator (KPI).

To determine a KPI for someone you are coaching (or for yourself), follow this process:

1. Rate yourself one to ten on how well you are setting and measuring your KPIs.
2. Pick one KPI to improve.
3. What's the current status?
4. What's the new goal status?
5. What's the specific action that you need to take?
6. What do you need to learn to be able to do it?

Here's how it works. Let's say that our salesperson is doing well converting leads into clients, but she needs more leads to reach her sales goals.

1. Both she and you should rate her performance from one to ten on how she is doing on getting leads now. Let's say you rated her a five. You and she both agree that because she loves people, is a bit of a "social butterfly," and gets most of

her leads now from one networking group, attending other networking functions is the way for her to get more leads.

2. The KPIs to improve would be number of networking functions attended per week and the number of new contacts made at each networking event.

3. So what's the current status? She is currently attending one networking function a week and getting four new business cards.

4. What's the new goal? She and you determine that attending three networking events each week and getting five new business cards at each one of those three events will be her key measurements. So her KPI is fifteen business cards from networking every single week.

5. What specific action does she need to take? She needs to find two more networking opportunities every single week and attend them with the idea of meeting at least five people at each event.

6. What does she need to learn? She needs to learn where those networking functions are and which ones are worth attending. She may also need to study and learn advanced networking strategies in order to gain prospects and referrals.

When determining the KPIs that you track for the people you coach, be mindful to keep a balance between the people considerations and the process indicators. For example, you may have worked for a person who was only concerned about the bottom line. The numbers were the only thing that mattered. Was it much fun? Was it a great place to work? Or was it a tough place to work? Likely, it was not a great place to work and likely there was a high turnover in employees.

On the other hand, you may have worked for someone who didn't really care about or track any numbers.

Likely, your results were not as good as they might have been. Find the balance. **The numbers don't lie.**

"Seek first to understand, then be understood,"
- Stephen Covey.

CHAPTER 7

EPIC PRINCIPLE #4: IT'S ABOUT THEM . . .

A great coach gets someone else to achieve something faster or better than they would have by working alone. To be successful, a coach has to commit "egocide." A lot of coaches are very skilled, smart, and proud of their own accomplishments and knowledge, so it is important for the coach to make sure their coaching focuses on their coachees. A great coach "makes it all about the people they coach (them)."

Here are a few concepts to master when focusing on your coachee:

1. Find Their Blind Spots

One of the great advantages you bring as a coach is being "outside looking in." When you go to a new restaurant, I'll bet you $100 that you'll be able to spot something the restaurant could do better. We all do this naturally.

Do the people you coach know what they need? My experience is that they probably don't. Everyone has "blind spots." When coaching, you need to recognize and use this natural talent.

I had a big blind spot when I gave my first presentation.

In my very first job after college, I was asked to give a presentation on behalf of our division to the other people in my training class in Chicago. There were about twenty of us, representing different divisions and sales offices from around the country, who were training together. Some were in the field and some of us worked in the manufacturing plants in marketing capacities. I happened to work in the "Pad Mount Transformer Division" in Jefferson City, Missouri.

For my presentation, I put together a slide deck. Do you remember slide projectors? Yes, this was back in the day of slide projectors. I worked hard on the presentation, getting it just right and adding some funny parts while still getting the information across to my class. I actually thought it was pretty good.

My boss and his boss happened to be in Chicago, and they came by to check on me and see the presentation. Pete, my boss's boss, and Don, my boss, asked me to dinner.

Pete said, "Bill, how do you think you did?"

"It could have been better."

And then he said, and I'll never forget it, "It was terrible."

He then went on, "But it's not your fault. Everyone in the division is giving terrible presentations. No one has actually been taught how to give a proper presentation. And we're going to fix that." So he did. He hired a presentation skills company to train all of us in the marketing division. We all got better, and thanks to Pete, I learned how to give presentations. Now presentations have become a large part of what I get to do. I think about Pete often with gratitude.[7]

But at the time of my first presentation, I couldn't see how bad I was. I had a blind spot. I needed outside feedback. As a participant, it's impossible to see the bigger picture. Professional athletes, actors, CEOs, and musicians all use videos, audios, and coaches to help them improve.

In football, you will always see some of the coaching staff in the sky box during the game relaying information down to the field via headset. Today, professional quarterbacks review the last series of plays visually on computers on the sidelines after they come off the field. They are all looking for that different viewpoint.

In my presentation example, I didn't know how to make it better, but in the presentation skills class, we videotaped everything and the whole class critiqued it, giving me many views. By the end of the class, I was crushing that presentation.

It's the same with the people you are coaching. All of them have blind spots. They think they know what they want, but they really don't know what they need. Help them find their blind spots.

A friend of mine says that "Left to their own devices, many people will make the bad decision. It's good for them to get advice from the outside."[8]

To help them overcome their blind spots, you need to use a 360-degree assessment. Instead of letting them assess themselves or just getting input from you, a 360-degree evaluation gets input from managers, other people on their same level, direct reports, and even

---

[7] I have one regret. I never took the opportunity to thank Pete, and now I can't because he died a number of years ago. If you have a mentor whom you haven't thanked, call them now and let them know what they mean to you. If by some strange coincidence any of Pete Chomyn's relatives read this, please know that I am grateful for how he helped me.
[8] Thanks Reggie Shropshire.

family members. We want to get input from as many viewpoints as we can, from 360 degrees around the person. Hence the name: 360-degree evaluation.

There are any number of stock 360-degree evaluations in the marketplace, and we have developed custom 360-degree evaluations for clients. Included in the workbook is an example of a custom 360-evaluation questionnaire. I recommend that you do a 360 evaluation with anyone you coach.[9]

2. Have a *Moment of Truth* Mentality

When entering a coaching session, you, as the coach, must have a *moment of truth* mentality. It's win or lose. It's like the athlete who has worked their entire life, their entire career, for that few seconds or few minutes they race for that gold medal.

As a kid, I wanted to be a basketball star. I spent a lot of time shooting in the driveway. I was physically in my driveway, but in my imagination, I was in the finals of The ACC Tournament.

I could hear the announcer saying, "We're down one with twelve seconds to go in the game. Gilliland is open. He gets the ball, he fakes left, he moves right around the top of the key. He shoots, and clank he misses."

"But wait, he was fouled on the play. He's got two shots at the free throw line. Gilliland needs to make both to win the game. He steps up calmly and drains the first one." This went on for hours. I played games in my head, practicing for that moment of glory. I never made it to the ACC, but I did make the winning shot in a playoff game in the sixth grade. That counts for something. Practice, practice, practice for that moment of truth.

---

[9] I can arrange a 360-degree evaluation or your company may have another provider.

In business, moments of truth are everywhere: the big meetings, the sales opportunity you've been working on for nine months, the negotiation, the final details of a merger or buyout. Every single coaching session is a moment of truth.

Your job is to help the people you coach get breakthroughs in their performance. You must be prepared mentally and physically to get them through the tough times and help them enjoy the good times. You will not help them get a breakthrough in every session, but you must be prepared to push and take them places mentally that they may not want to go.

In coaching people over the years, I have found that from time to time, it is easy to go through the motions of coaching: to be physically on a call or at a meeting, but not to be there 100% mentally. This is not fair to the coachee and will yield less than optimal results. Be in the moment and recognize that a moment of truth could happen at any time.

One must reset before each coaching session and be ready to give one's all to each coachee. A good mantra is "it's all about them. It's now or never. I am giving them my all. Now is the moment of truth that will change their life forever."

Every single session is important. Understand the importance of now, be present, and have that *moment of truth* mentality.

3. If You Think it, Ask it

Coaching is a bit intuitive. The good news is that we, as humans, are naturally intuitive. We know instinctively when someone walks in the room whether or not they are in a bad mood or a good mood.

As a coach, open yourself up to what you are sensing and become comfortable asking the tough questions. I've learned to listen carefully, and if a question pops into my head, I ask it.

Early on in my coaching career, I was coaching a small group of business owners, helping them price their products and services. A web design and marketing client told me others were beating her in price and she needed to be the lowest price to get the business. Naturally, lower prices hurt her profits. I asked her, "Is that the way you want to be known? As the cheapest in town?" She immediately was embarrassed and said, "No, I don't."

And that was the breakthrough moment for her. She realized that she needed to compete on value or service, really anything besides price. And now, she has become very successful.

Ask the hard questions. If you think it, ask it.

Know your client and yourself.

In addition to 360-degree evaluations, behavioral assessments and personality tests like DISC, Myers-Briggs, and Profiles XT are useful in coaching your people. I like DISC, which tells people how they prefer to behave, and VAK (Visual, Auditory, Kinesthetic), which tells people how they prefer to learn. They are simple, quick to administer, and insightful. Both assessments are useful in coaching people.

You may find that assessments may help you in specific situations or help you learn more about yourself and your coachees. I find that a lot of companies will administer assessments, have a fun workshop or debrief on them, and then put them in a drawer somewhere. If your company uses a specific assessment methodology already and it works, use that in your coaching.

4. Be a Role Model

Inspiration is the third building block in the EPIC Formula. Positive role models inspire and educate. Negative role models disgust us. Coach John Wooden said, "Being a role model is the most powerful form of educating."

As a coach, the people you coach will pick up intuitively on who you are and what you are doing, and often miss what you say. One of my clients says that being a poor role model "is like telling your kids not to drink and drive and then driving around with a beer in your hand." Your kids are going to do what you do, not what you say to do.

And so will your clients. Be aware that the people you coach are watching. Early in my coaching career, I had trouble getting some of my clients to complete their quarterly plans. After thinking about it, I realized that it was unreasonable for me to ask them to complete a plan when I didn't have a plan. I never told them I didn't have a plan—they sensed it. I completed my plan and shared it with my clients, and amazingly, they all completed their plans.

5. Be a Lifelong Learner

Coaching is teaching. And teaching is educating. So part of coaching is educating. Being an education role model means knowing enough to ask the right questions. If your coachee learns more than you, you will lose them as a client. In order to keep your coaching relevant and outward focused, develop your own education plan and stick to it. Be a lifelong learner.

6. End Coaching Sessions on a High Note

Often in coaching, you will have to ask tough questions and take them to some deep and retrospective places. Coaching sessions often become emotional with crying from time to time. You will need to apply pressure, and when your people breakthrough, there will be an emotional release. It can be draining on you and the people you coach.

Sometimes this discussion is about something that has happened in the past. But regardless what brought the session to its emotional state, it is important to flip the discussion to something positive and forward-looking by the end of a session. You want the person to leave with confidence, knowing they can accomplish the goals you have set.

Have you ever watched a sports coach during a timeout? Often the coach has called the timeout because they are not happy with how his or her players are performing. So the coach usually starts chastising them a little bit, but by the end of the timeout, the coach will flip the narrative to something like, "OK here's our strategy; let's get this done. 1, 2, 3 break." The team leaves the huddle on a high note.

When you do this, the people you coach will leave the session inspired. Make sure they have specific goals and instructions moving forward and make sure to end the session on a high note.

7. Get Results with Consistency.

In any coaching relationship, it is important that you and your coachee must "be climbing the same wall."

Start any coaching assignment with an alignment process to ensure you and the people you coach are all working to achieve the same goals; the person you coach is aligned with themselves; and you are aligned with them. This process should be completed at least once a year with each person you are coaching.

At the end of a good alignment process the person you are coaching will understand the vision, their goals, their learning plan, and they will have at least a quarterly plan in place. There is a brief overview of alignments in the workbook, but I believe that you should learn this process from us or another ActionCOACH.

Use a Pre-Coaching Session Focus Sheet

For each session, your coachee should show up with or send ahead of time a "focus sheet." The focus sheet will help them be prepared for the session with you and keep them focused on what is important. This form can be modified depending on your specific situation, but should at least have a recap of the weekly goals and how they did at accomplishing those goals. A sample focus sheet is in the workbook.

Use Scripting

Each coaching session should follow the same basic format or script. Once again, the script may vary depending on the situation. A simple script includes the basic questions:

- What did you accomplish?
- What were your wins?
- What were your challenges?
- What did you learn?
- What help do you need from me?
- What are your goals for next week?

Stick to the Same Bat Time. Same Bat Channel

When I was a kid, before the era of binge-watching television programs, *Batman* was one of the hottest programs. The program would always end with "Tune in next week. Same Bat Time, Same Bat Channel." Coaching sessions work best if they happen at the same day and time each week. You'll form a rhythm that will create good habits.

8. Look Forward

Coaching is about moving your coachee forward. Always leave the people you are coaching with a clear list of things to accomplish for the next week and a clear understanding of the strategies and tactics that you will work on sometime in the future. In each coaching session, you will review the list of goals from the previous coaching session, noting accomplishments, challenges, and learnings. Then you will establish priorities and goals to be accomplished before the next session.

This process often focuses us on details and tactics. In order to maintain a forward focused mindset, you must always tie the tactics back to the individual strategy that your coachee is currently working toward. In addition, you must also tie in each strategy to the long-term, bigger-picture vision or dream.

9. Collect Ideas, but Focus on the Priorities

You will see that coachees often get "shiny object syndrome" and will flit from new idea to new idea. Without focus and follow through, your coachee will likely want to start working on the latest new idea and drop the current strategies. The hard work is staying on plan and finishing.

When great ideas and strategies come up in coaching sessions, put those new ideas in a long-term list to pull out later—after completing the current priorities. I call this long-term list "The Parking Lot." I have another friend who calls it "The Someday, Maybe File."

Experience has shown me that most people can only work on three major goals or projects at one time. Any tasks, projects, or strategies that don't help us achieve our three current goals should go in the "Parking Lot" or the garbage can.

10. Application and Accountability

Every session spend some time discussing how your coachee is applying the strategies discussed and what kind of results they are achieving. By having regular coaching sessions at the same time and following the same script, you have built in accountability as part of your coaching system.

"Who you are is speaking so loudly that I can't hear what you were saying."
-Ralph Waldo Emerson

CHAPTER 8

EPIC PRINCIPLE #5 - RELATIONSHIPS MATTER

The coaching relationship is unique and special. In the quote above, Ralph Waldo Emerson points out that the way we act, our body language, our tonality, and our congruency matters so much that the people we coach can become deaf to what we are saying.

You have no doubt experienced a time when you felt that someone's demeanor just didn't match their words. Or a time you instinctively knew when a friend said they were "OK" that they were not.

This is amplified in any coaching relationship. If "life is a mirror," the coaching relationship is one of those magnifying mirrors at the amusement park. When in the role of "coach," you must be absolutely true and congruent. If not, the person or persons you are coaching will sense your incongruence and will interpret the feeling they are sensing as insincerity. It's important to remember that who you truly are will determine the success you get with your people.

In his book *The Referral of a Lifetime*,[10] Tim Templeton outlines a simple method to determine what type of referral program a person should implement based on who they are and how others see them. I have found this model useful for building coaching relationships as well. Understanding the tendencies of the people you coach will make you a better coach.

It's a simple model really. Just have your coachee answer two questions:

- How do people view them initially? Are they more "relational" or "businesslike"?
- What are their natural tendencies in business—relational or businesslike?

There are four combinations. People fall into one of four categories: relational-relational, relational-business, business-relational, and business-business.

How Others View You	Your Natural Tendency
Relational	Relational
Relational	Business
Business	Relational
Business	Business

If a person is **relational-relational**, they love building relationships. They will only think of relationships. So when first meeting someone new that person will immediately get to know as much about them as possible and work hard to build a personal relationship. And they will continue to build that relationship without much regard to the business ramifications.

---

[10] *Templeton, Timothy L. The Referral of a Lifetime: The Networking System That Produces Bottom-line Results, Every Day! San Francisco, CA: Berrett-Koehler, 2005.*

A relational-relational person will be very strong at the people KPIs but will likely be averse to the hard numbers. Coach them on how to use their natural relationship interests and skills to get business results.

If a person is **relational-business**, then they will start out truly interested in building a relationship, but when the discussion turns to business, they will begin to think strategically. They will start by building a relationship first, and then work their way around to the business at hand.

When coaching a relational-business person, you'll want to spend some time getting to know them before you ask them to complete any real work. Then move to the strategies and tactics they need to implement

If a person is **business-relational**, they are the exact opposite of relational-business. They prefer to be businesslike in the beginning of a relationship and move slowly to deepen that relationship.

When coaching a business-relational person, get down to business first, and as you work with them over time, you'll be able to get to know them in a deeper manner and build stronger relationships. I'm business-relational. I tend to start out all business and focus on getting things done, and then as I actually get to know people, I build close friendships over time.

Finally, if a person is **business-business**, they are all business, all the time. They couldn't care less about building close personal relationships. They will not invest time in building relationships unless they can justify it in some businesslike way.

In coaching a business-business person, stay strictly to the business at hand. There is no need to ever get touchy-feely. Just stick to the script and hold them highly accountable. It is important to help them understand the impact that their business mentality will have on others.

As a coach, you will want to be a bit of a chameleon. You will need to adapt your style to that of the person you are coaching. For example, let's say you tend to be business-business, and you are coaching a relational-relational person. To avoid a complete disconnect, you will need to soften your approach to achieve any outcome.

Action Step: Determine your style. Which of the four styles are you? Then understand the style of the person you are coaching. Armed with this, the 360-degree evaluation, assessments, and your instincts and experience, you will find success building your business and maybe a few personal relationships.

CHAPTER 9

CONCLUSION

You now understand the four EPIC Building Blocks for developing your coaching program: Education, Planning, Inspiration, and Commitment. Be successful in these areas of coaching and you'll achieve great results with the people you coach.

You have also learned the five EPIC principles designed to give you more context and to help you become a better coach: "You're So Fine"; "To Have EPIC wins, You Must Have EPIC Fails"; "The Numbers Don't Lie"; "It's About Them..."; and "Relationships Matter." Commit to understanding the content and the context of these principles.

Understand these principles, but understanding without application is folly. The only way to get better is to actually experience being the coach.

So here are a few things to do:
1. Do come to each session prepared.
2. Do know your clients DISC, VAC, and relational-behavioral profile.
3. Do coach to both results and the people side of things.

4. Do keep it professional.
5. Do use the concept of the hats. In other words, if you're changing from coach to friend to manager to boss, whatever it is, you need to let the people know which hat you are currently wearing.
6. Do remember that you are there for them.
7. Do have a moment of truth mentality.
8. Do respect that relationships matter.
9. Do remember that you are coaching a person.
10. Do understand your differences.
11. Do expect results.
12. Do remember that your actions and your tones will say more than the actual words ever will.

Coaching is something you must practice. You can always be better.

Go ahead. Get started. Your next step is to download and complete the free workbook at: https://billgilliland.biz/epicworkbook.

With the workbook, you actually have all the tools necessary to implement *The Coach Approach* in your business.

Whether you take this approach alone or whether you'd like to work with our team to implement this program, know that *The Coach Approach* will help you get there faster.

SELF-PUBLISHING SCHOOL

NOW IT'S YOUR TURN

Discover the EXACT 3-step blueprint you need to become a bestselling author in 3 months.

Self-Publishing School helped me, and now I want them to help you with this FREE WEBINAR!

Even if you're busy, bad at writing, or don't know where tostart, you CAN write a bestseller.

With tools and experience across a variety niches and professions, Self-Publishing School is the <u>only</u> resource you need to take your book to the finish line!

DON'T WAIT

Watch this FREE WEBINAR now, and
Say "YES" to becoming a bestseller:
https://xe172.isrefer.com/go/sps4fta-vts/bookbrosinc6182

ABOUT THE AUTHOR

Bill Gilliland

One of Bill's oldest childhood memories is playing hide and seek with his brother and sister among the clothing racks in the retail stores that his father managed. There he learned lessons like "do what you say you are going to do" and "always put yourself in the other person's shoes" which have served him well on his business journey.

Since then, he has owned businesses in industries ranging from automation to coaching and from poultry to transportation. Twelve years ago, Bill found his true calling in coaching other business owners to success. Bill has worked with hundreds of business owners to achieve EPIC business results while also helping them reach their personal goals. As he watched his best clients become coaches within their own organizations, Bill realized that good coaching created more good coaches. Bill is now on a mission to help business owners and their organizations develop coaches and coaching programs from within.

Bill is currently one on the top ActionCOACH business coaches in the world, speaks on a wide range of business topics, and loves to teach business owners how to develop and implement coaching programs inside their businesses using the EPIC principles.

Bill lives in Montreat, NC with his wife of 34 years, Lynn. They have two grown sons. In his spare time, Bill enjoys golf, fly-fishing, reading books on business and theology, and pretty much doing anything outdoors with his sons.

Have Bill Address Your Organization

To have Bill address your organization, please contact him at https://billgilliland.biz/contact or email him at williamgilliland@actioncoach.com.

To Receive your Free Workboook

To download the workbook that accompanies this book, visit https://billgilliland.biz/epicworkbook

To Set Up Your Free Strategy Session

You will find more information on *The Coach Approach* and a link to set up a free strategy session at https://billgilliland.biz/